THE RELAPSE/RECOVERY GRID

About the pamphlet:

Terence T. Gorski gives us positive steps we can take to prevent relapse and continue personal growth. Based on Gorski's six developmental stages of recovery, the pamphlet shows us relapse warning signs and gives us an action plan for living a richly rewarding, chemical-free life.

About the author:

Terence T. Gorski, M.A., C.A.C., is a nationally recognized author, lecturer, workshop leader, and an acknowledged leader in the chemical dependency and codependency fields. His comprehensive approach to recovery, based on his nearly twenty years of clinical experience, has revolutionized the field of relapse prevention. Gorski's pioneering work in relapse prevention has helped thousands of chemically dependent people to achieve sobriety. His ability to explain complex recovery principles in an entertaining and easy-to-understand way has made him a popular public speaker. Thousands of people use his practical approach to relationship-building in recovery. As president of The CENAPS Corporation (The Center For Applied Sciences) in Hazel Crest, Illinois, he has provided research, training, and consultation services to numerous treatment centers.

THE RELAPSE/RECOVERY GRID

Terence T. Gorski

HazeLDeN

First published June 1989.

ISBN: 0-89486-544-7

Printed in the United States of America.

INTRODUCTION

This pamphlet will guide you on the path that has been taken by many persons who are in recovery from alcoholism and other drug dependency. This process is based on the Twelve Steps of Alcoholics Anonymous (A.A.). But we will view the recovery process from a broader perspective too. We will integrate the A.A. program with procedures from professional addiction counseling.

Recovery from chemical dependency is a process, not an event. The recovery process begins when chemically dependent people first recognize they are having problems because of their alcohol or other drug use. The goal is reached when they can live a meaningful and comfortable life without the need for alcohol or other drugs. The road between these points is long, difficult, and often confusing. Only in recent years has research begun to describe the process used by people who successfully achieve a meaningful and comfortable sobriety.

ADDICTIVE DISEASE AND THE RECOVERY PROCESS

It is the *progressive* process of addiction that creates the need for recovery in the first place. Chemical addiction begins when a person predisposed to chemical dependency begins using mood-altering chemicals. The chemicals provide a unique state of well-being called euphoria, which allows a person to feel better without having to think better or act better. The chemical use, whether it is alcohol or other mood-altering drugs, allows the chemically dependent person to bypass the normal steps of emotional growth.

Emotionally mature people recognize that feeling good is linked to what they think and do. They accept that in order to feel good they must think productive thoughts and take productive action.

Chemically dependent people learn how to feel better (experience euphoria) by using alcohol or other mood-altering chemicals. When euphoria (feeling good) can be achieved simply by using alcohol or other drugs, emotional growth stops. Since there is no need to think or to act more responsibly to feel better, chemically

1

dependent people stop learning nonchemical methods of managing their feelings and emotions.

The frequent use of alcohol or other drugs to achieve euphoria often results in the development of tolerance to them. As a person learns to tolerate the mood-altering chemicals, it takes more to achieve the same effect. As a result, people begin using more frequently. Heavy and frequent use of alcohol or other drugs leads to dependence. People who are dependent get uncomfortable when they stop using.

This discomfort is caused by a combination of physical, psychological, and social factors.

- Physically, withdrawal from alcohol and other drugs creates symptoms of agitation and discomfort.

- Psychologically, withdrawal creates anxiety. The drug on which the chemically dependent person relies, in order to cope with stress, is no longer available.

- Socially, withdrawal feels uncomfortable. A chemically dependent person's entire social network has been organized around his or her progressive alcohol and drug use. And, when use stops, social pressure is put on the person to use again.

Where Recovery Begins

When chemically dependent people begin having problems that interfere with their ability to live the way they would normally choose to, they are forced to attempt problem-solving strategies. From this point on, they are in the recovery process, although they may continue to use alcohol and drugs for some time.

Recovery can be described as a progressive process that unfolds through six stages. Each stage has a number of recovery tasks that need to be completed. There are specific skills or competencies a recovering person needs to develop during each stage. If certain tasks are skipped, people are not prepared to meet the future challenge of recovery. They develop a high risk for relapse and often experience a low quality of sobriety, marked by chronic stress and living problems.

THE RELAPSE/RECOVERY GRID

Throughout the discussion of the recovery and relapse process, you are encouraged to refer to *The Relapse/Recovery Grid* that appears on pages 4-5. This grid describes the process of recovery, identifies common stuck points, reviews both *relapse-prone* and *recovery-prone* styles for coping with those stuck points, and, finally, reviews what is happening when there is a relapse.

The top half of *The Relapse/Recovery Grid* shows the six phases of recovery. This is a developmental model of recovery. *Developmental* simply means starting with simple tasks, learning them well, and moving on to more complex and sophisticated tasks. A *model* is a tool for learning. This suggested guideline can help recovering people understand what they will face in the future and identify strengths and weaknesses in their current recovery programs.

Recovery is learning to live a meaningful and comfortable life without the need for chemicals. Recovery is more than not using alcohol or other drugs. It is growth and development during which people learn to fully "actualize" themselves. *Actualization* is making something real through action. Recovery is the process of making ourselves real through the thoughts and the actions we take. Let's review in detail each of the recovery tasks on the grid.

I. Transition	II. Stabilization	III. Early Recovery
1. Develop motivating problems.	1. Recognition of the need for help.	1. Full conscious recognition of addicitve disease.
2. Failure of normal problem-solving.	2. Recovery from immediate after-effects.	2. Full acceptance and integration of the addiction.
3. Failure of controlled use strategies.	3. Interrupting pathological preoccupation.	3. Learning nonchemical coping skills.
4. Acceptance of need for abstinence.	4. Learning nonchemical stress management methods.	4. Short-term social stabilization.
	5. Developing hope and motivation.	5. Developing a sobriety-centered value system.

(Start of Relapse
Process)

Coping With
1. Denial and evasion: *(The relapse-prone style)* a. Evade/deny the stuck point. b. Stress. c. Compulsive behavior. d. Avoid others. e. Problems. f. Evade/deny new problems. MEMORY PEG = ESCAPE

High-Risk Factors	Trigger Events	Internal Dysfunction
1. High-stress personality.	1. High-stress thoughts.	1. Difficulty in thinking clearly.
2. High-risk lifestyle.	2. Painful emotions.	2. Difficulty in managing feelings and emotions.
3. Social conflict or change.	3. Painful memories.	3. Difficulty in remembering things.
4. Poor health maintenance.	4. Stressful situations.	4. Difficulty in sleeping restfully.
5. Other illness.	5. Stressful interactions with other people.	5. Difficulty in managing stress.
6. Inadequate recovery program.		6. Difficulty with physical coordination.
		7. Shame, guilt, hopelessness.
		8. Return of denial.

For Further Information Contact

Recovery: The Relapse/Recovery Grid
Gorski Copyright, T. Gorski, 1987 (Revised May 1987)

IV. Middle Recovery	V. Late Recovery	VI. Maintenance.
1. Resolving the demoralization crisis.	1. Recognizing the effects of childhood problems on sobriety.	1. Maintain a recovery program.
2. Repairing addiction-caused social damage.	2. Learning about family-of-origin issues.	2. Effective day-to-day coping.
3. Establishing a self-regulated recovery program.	3. Conscious examination of childhood.	3. Continued growth and development.
4. Establishing lifestyle balance.	4. Application to adult living.	4. Effective coping with life transitions.
5. Management of change.	5. Change in lifestyle.	

s In Recovery

Recogniton and problem solving:
(The recovery-prone style)
a. **Recognizing** a problem exists.
b. **Accept** that it is okay to have problems.
c. **Detach** to gain perspective.
d. **Ask** for help.
e. **Respond** with action when prepared.

MEMORY PEG = RADAR

(Return of the
Recovery Process)

External Dysfunction	Loss of Control	Lapse/Relapse
1. Avoidance and defensive behavior.	1. Poor judgment.	1. Initial use of alcohol or other drugs.
2. Crisis building.	2. Inability to take action.	2. Severe shame, guilt, and remorse.
3. Immobilization.	3. Inability to resist destructive impulses.	3. Loss of control over use.
4. Confusion and overreaction.	4. Conscious recognition of the severity of loss of control.	4. Development of health and life problems.
5. Depression.	5. Option reduction.	
	6. Emotional or physical collapse.	

STAGE I
TRANSITION

The first phase of recovery is *transition*. This is a time when chemically dependent people believe they are "social drinkers" or "recreational drug users" who are capable of controlling their use. They are aware that they have problems, but have not entered treatment or become involved with a Twelve Step program because they don't believe they need to. At the end of this stage, they accept their chemical dependency; they accept that they cannot control their use. To come to this acceptance, most chemically dependent people experience the following:

1. Develop Motivating Problems*

As we learned earlier, the transition period begins when chemically dependent people first recognize that their problems are becoming progressively more serious. These are *motivating problems* because they motivate people to take action. Initially, these problems are only a nuisance, but eventually they become so bad they interfere with a normal life, or preferred lifestyle — "life the way I want to live it."

Most people don't take problems seriously until they interfere with their preferred way of living. Chemically dependent people are no different. They ignore or rationalize problems for as long as possible. Because chemical dependency is progressive, the problems naturally get worse. Chemically dependent people can't believe their problems are related to alcohol or drug use, so they attempt to solve their problems while ignoring the obvious cause.

---

* Editor's note: The concepts discussed for each area are numbered to correspond with *The Relapse/Recovery Grid.*

2. Failure of Normal Problem-Solving

Normal problem-solving involves identifying problems, examining options for solving them, and putting one of those options into practice. Ordinarily, this type of problem-solving works well. It doesn't work well for problems created by chemical dependency. At this point, chemically dependent people don't realize the true source of their problems, and their efforts at problem-solving fail repeatedly.

3. Failure of Controlled Use Strategies

Repeated failure to solve problems causes chemically dependent people to realize that their problems must be related to their chemical use. But at this stage, they still don't believe they are *addicted.* They still believe that they are normal, social, recreational users who are capable of control. They believe they must have problems because they use too much, too often, or they use the wrong kind of drug. The solution, in their minds, is easy: control how much, how often, and what kind of drug they use. Because addiction is a disease marked by loss of control, these attempts fail.

4. Acceptance of the Need for Abstinence

Repeated failures at controlling their chemical use finally force chemically dependent people to recognize that they are not social or recreational users who are capable of control. They recognize they have lost control. When chemically dependent people can finally accept this, they are ready to understand that total abstinence from alcohol and drugs is the only way to resolve their life problems.

At this point, the stage I call *transition* is complete. The person has surrendered to the reality that controlled use of alcohol or other drugs is impossible. There is a need to live a lifestyle of abstinence.

STAGE II
STABILIZATION

The second recovery phase is *stabilization*. The primary goal of this stage is to recuperate from damage caused by the addiction. This can take from six to eighteen months. As a general rule, a person will need one month recuperation time for every year of heavy use of alcohol or other drugs.

The Twelve Step program of Alcoholics Anonymous has three primary tools to help a recovering person through this time:

• *Attending meetings.*

It is often suggested that a new member attend ninety meetings in ninety days. Attending Twelve Step meetings gets a person in contact with other sober people.

• *Finding a sponsor.*

A sponsor is someone more knowledgeable about the program, who has longer sobriety, and who can provide help during rough times.

• *Learning slogans.*

The new member is taught a number of slogans, such as Easy Does It, One Day at a Time, Live and Let Live, There Is No Problem So Bad That a Drink Won't Make It Worse, and Turn It Over and Leave It There. These slogans interrupt "addictive thinking." They have also been described as "thought-terminating cliches." They can help stop preoccupation with using chemicals.

Most recovering people move through the stabilization stage by completing the following:

1. Recognition of the Need for Help

One of the biggest problems chemically dependent people have is with asking for help. Most addicted people believe they

8

need to be self-sufficient; thus, they often attempt abstinence for the first time without asking for help. They are typically overwhelmed by symptoms of physical and psychological withdrawal, social pressures, and an avalanche of problems created by their addictive use. These solo efforts at recovery typically fail. They realize they cannot maintain abstinence by themselves. When chemically dependent people are ready to seek help, they often get involved in the appropriate Twelve Step program, such as A.A. for alcohol problems or Narcotics Anonymous (N.A.) for drug problems. Some seek professional counseling. Others admit themselves to rehabilitation programs. One of the best sources of help is a certified alcohol and drug abuse counselor who can formulate an appropriate treatment plan.

Most people find that stabilization is safer and easier if they participate in both a Twelve Step recovery program and professional counseling. I call this the "Twelve Step Plus" approach. Whatever the source of outside help, the goal is to regain control of thinking, feelings, judgment, and behavior. This involves entering a protective environment to recover from the immediate aftereffects of addiction, called withdrawal.

2. Recovery from Immediate Aftereffects

Withdrawal is a direct consequence of physical and psychological dependence on chemicals. Addicted people have used alcohol or other drugs heavily for such a long time that they have the ability to function while intoxicated; their brain chemistry has adjusted to intoxication as normal, and to sobriety as abnormal. To function well, the body now requires mood-altering chemicals, or symptoms of dysfunction occur. The symptoms are both short- and long-term. Short-term symptoms usually clear up in three to five days and include insomnia, agitation, irritability, and tremors. Long-term withdrawal symptoms, which can take from six to eighteen months to clear, include difficulty in thinking clearly, managing feelings, remembering things, and sleeping restfully. During times of low stress the symptoms lessen; in times of high

9

stress, the symptoms return. During extended periods of high stress, people may become accident prone or develop severe symptoms that can lead to a physical or emotional collapse.

Recovery from both long- and short-term withdrawal requires abstinence from alcohol and other drugs, knowledge of how to manage withdrawal symptoms in a sober state, and proper medical care. It also requires a structured recovery program that includes education, Twelve Step group involvement, and proper diet and exercise to relieve stress and help the brain chemistry return to normal. Once these symptoms are under control most chemically dependent people need to confront their preoccupation with chemicals.

3. Interrupting Pathological Preoccupation

In the stabilization period, chemically dependent people are often self-destructively preoccupied with alcohol and drug use. Their addictive preoccupation comes from a combination of

- awfulizing sobriety,
- euphoric recall,
- positive expectancy,
- obsession,
- compulsion, and
- craving.

Awfulizing sobriety is the process of consciously focusing on the negative aspects of sobriety while blocking out the positive. This causes one to believe that sobriety is awful or terrible.

Euphoric recall is the process of consciously focusing on only the positive memories of alcohol and other drug-using experiences while blocking out the negative, allowing people to believe that chemical use was good.

Euphoric recall leads to the belief that chemical use may be good in the future. Since alcohol or other drug use brought

10

pain-free pleasure and relief in the past, it is only "reasonable" to believe it will bring pleasure and relief in the future. This is *positive expectancy,* and it sets the stage for obsession.

Addictive *obsession* is the inability to stop thinking about the positive effects of alcohol and drug use. Recovering people may spend a great deal of time thinking about how good chemical use was ("the good old days"), and how awful it is that they can't experience this in the future ("the dreary days of recovery").

Thinking about the positive effects of alcohol or other drug use will eventually trigger an emotional reaction: *compulsion.* The compulsion will be an irrational urge to use alcohol or other drugs even though it is apparent that the result will be harmful. If the compulsion is strong and persists for a time, brain chemistry will trigger a *craving,* a physical hunger for the alcohol or other drugs. The body actually craves or "needs" the chemical. When craving occurs, many people feel physical discomfort like the withdrawal they experienced shortly after they stopped using chemicals.

People who maintain abstinence learn how to interrupt addictive preoccupation. They stop awfulizing sobriety by appreciating the benefits of being straight and sober. They examine their past use to stop euphoric recall. They stop thinking about how wonderful it would be to use chemicals in the future. They talk openly about their obsessions, compulsions, and cravings with other people who are supportive of their recovery.

4. Learning Nonchemical Stress Management Methods

A big part of stabilization is learning how to manage stress without alcohol and drugs. During active addiction, most chemically dependent people learned a stress management formula like this:

Stress + Alcohol or other Drugs = Relaxation.

When the alcohol or other drug is gone, no method for coping with stress remains. Until new ways of coping are learned, stress

11

will build until chemically dependent people feel that they need to use alcohol and drugs or else they will go crazy.

5. Developing Hope and Motivation

As chemically dependent people make progress, they begin to believe that recovery is possible. They learn this by meeting and talking with other chemically dependent people who are more advanced in their recovery. They are now feeling better, having overcome the worst symptoms of withdrawal and addictive preoccupation.

By now, they believe in the recovery process as the way to get well. If others have done it, they know they can do it too. They are willing to invest time, energy, and resources into the recovery process.

STAGE III
EARLY RECOVERY

Now it is time for the recovering person to begin the process of internal change. *Early recovery* is when a chemically dependent person begins changing his or her entire belief system.

In early recovery, many chemically dependent people believe addiction is a moral weakness. They believe that they became addicted because they were immoral, weak, or emotionally ill. By the end of this stage, most will have come to believe their addiction is a physical disease that caused psychological, social, and spiritual problems. They will understand that shame and guilt are feelings associated with this disease and must be resolved for continuing sobriety to be possible.

During early recovery, most recovering people work the first seven Steps of the A.A. program. These deal with internal change. What follows are Steps One through Seven with my interpretation included after each Step.*

---

* Editor's note: The author's interpretation of the Twelve Steps is his own, and not A.A.'s interpretation.

12

Step One: We admitted we were powerless over alcohol — that our lives had become unmanageable.

I recognize and accept that I'm addicted to alcohol and other drugs and that my addiction has caused serious life problems. I can no longer safely use alcohol or other drugs, and I will need help in staying abstinent. I can't recover alone.

Step Two: Came to believe that a Power greater than ourselves could restore us to sanity.

There is help available from other people and a Higher Power.

Step Three: Made a decision to turn our will and our lives over to the care of God *as we understood Him.*

I'll ask for help from this Higher Power and follow directions.

Step Four: Made a searching and fearless moral inventory of ourselves.

I will evaluate my current strengths and weaknesses so I can build upon my strengths and overcome my weaknesses.

Step Five: Admitted to God, to ourselves, and to another human being the exact nature of our wrongs.

I will discuss my self-evaluation with at least one other person and listen to the feedback.

Step Six: Were entirely ready to have God remove all these defects of character.

I will become willing to do the work necessary to overcome these weaknesses by paying attention to the daily pain and problems that they cause.

Step Seven: Humbly asked Him to remove our shortcomings.

*I will receive from my Higher Power the courage, strength, and hope to overcome these weaknesses by going to any lengths to learn how to resolve them.**

---

* The Steps are reprinted with permission of A.A. World Services, Inc., New York, N.Y., from *Alcoholics Anonymous* (Third Edition), 59-60. The complete Twelve Steps of A.A. appear in Appendix One.

1. Full Conscious Recognition of Addictive Disease

People in early recovery need to recognize that chemical dependency is a disease. This task is completed intellectually. For chemically dependent people, the task involves having an accurate understanding of the nature of addiction, applying that understanding to themselves, and acknowledging that they have this disease. Their recognition is not complete until they are capable of defending, to those who might try to convince them otherwise, the belief that they are addicted.

2. Full Acceptance and Integration of the Addiction

Another important part of the early recovery process is acceptance, which occurs on an emotional level; it is a gut feeling. Chemically dependent people must resolve the emotional pain that follows them into sobriety. To do this, they must identify their feelings and talk about them. This helps resolve their shame and guilt, and helps get rid of negative feelings about their drinking or using past.

3. Learning Nonchemical Coping Skills

Recovering people need to learn new coping skills, without alcohol and other drugs. Most chemically dependent people have never learned how to do this. During early recovery, they begin to find ways of coping with everyday problems. They also learn how to identify and deal with both pleasant and unpleasant emotions. Coping with life in a sober state allows self-esteem and a sense of inner security to return.

4. Short-Term Social Stabilization

Most chemically dependent people are in crisis when they stop alcohol and drug use. They may be at risk of divorce, termination from work, or legal action. These situations must be stabilized for the time being. This is not a time for permanent, long-term solutions, but a time for emergency action to prevent future losses.

5. Developing a Sobriety-Centered Value System

As recovering people become more skillful at living, their values change and they see that using chemicals is not a good way of life. They gradually lose their desire for chemicals and become grateful for recovery. At this point, they have completed their early recovery. Many people now say, "I am grateful for my addiction because it brought me to a new and better place in life."

STAGE IV
MIDDLE RECOVERY

As they enter *middle recovery,* most people are regularly attending Twelve Step meetings and possibly therapy. They are coping on a day-to-day basis but do not yet have a well-balanced and satisfying lifestyle. Things are better than they were during the active addiction; still, a great deal more work needs to be done.

1. Resolving the Demoralization Crisis

It can be demoralizing — after six to eighteen months of sobriety — to realize that there is more work to do. After putting forth much effort to change patterns of thinking, feeling, and behaving it is discouraging to learn this is not the end of the recovery process, but the beginning of more work. Many recovering people resist further growth. They attend Twelve Step meetings, focus on the

15

first three Steps, and resist other change. They stop growing. Others have the courage to move ahead. They are willing to confront reality, to do the work required for a balanced lifestyle.

2. Repairing Addiction-Caused Social Damage

During middle recovery, people make major changes in their lives. The primary goal is external change or lifestyle reconstruction. Changes are made in important areas such as marriage, relationships with children, social lives, and careers. Damage done to these areas is repaired. At this time, chemically dependent people need rigorous honesty in every area of their lives. They learn to function effectively and meaningfully on the job, at home, and with friends. They adjust their lifestyle to fit their emerging personal values. It is during this stage that most people work Steps Eight and Nine of the A.A. program. What follows are A.A. Steps Eight and Nine followed by my shorthand interpretation:

Step Eight: Made a list of all persons we had harmed, and became willing to make amends to them all.
We identified the people that were hurt by our addiction and became willing to repair the damage we had done to them.

Step Nine: Made direct amends to such people wherever possible, except when to do so would injure them or others.
We sincerely tried to fix the damage caused by our addiction when it was possible to do so.

It is not enough to stop using chemicals and to go to meetings, if we refuse to change other areas of our lives. The Steps suggest practicing the principles of recovery in *all* of our affairs.

3. Establishing a Self-Regulated Recovery Program

As past damage to relationships is being repaired, many recovering people discover other areas of life that need change for a

16

comfortable sobriety. One man, for example, realized he was unhappy in his work. As a salesman, he found a way he could drink the way he wanted and still earn a living. When he became sober, he found the job unsatisfying for him, but he had no other job skills. He needed to reduce the A.A. meetings he attended each week from five to four so he could go to a career counseling session.

One woman was unhappy in her marriage. Although she had made amends to her husband, she was dissatisfied with their lack of intimacy. They discussed this and decided to enter marriage counseling. She reduced the A.A. meetings she attended each week from four to three so they could get counseling and so she would have more private time with her husband.

A person must be willing to go to any lengths to attain a balanced lifestyle. This often means modifying a recovery program to include other forms of education or therapy that supplement the Twelve Step program.

4. Establishing Lifestyle Balance

Many recovering people find they live a one-dimensional life, narrowly focused with little variety. Some work, go to meetings, and do little else. Or perhaps they raise a family and go to meetings, and have no other outlet. Middle recovery calls for balance and development of several interests. To achieve lifestyle balance, a person begins to examine the areas of personal habits, family, work, and social life. Maintaining personal health involves a comfortable balance of all of these areas. After investing time and energy, most recovering people can have a meaningful and productive job, a satisfying marriage or love relationship, a good relationship with one's family, and a solid recovery program with a good sponsor. They also can make numerous friends in the program, and develop friendships with others who are not involved in the Twelve Step program.

5. Management of Change

Recovering people learn that stable recovery does not mean *problem-free* recovery. It means learning how to manage the problems of life without becoming unduly upset. This day-to-day discipline is part of what recovering people learn in middle recovery. Working the Tenth Step helps us achieve such discipline.

Step 10: Continued to take personal inventory and when we were wrong promptly admitted it.

We made a commitment to stay conscious of our behavior and its consequences. When we became aware of negative consequences, we found the behaviors causing them and changed those behaviors.

Recovering people are learning the difference between thoughts, feelings, and actions. They learn how to think a problem through, identify and resolve any feelings about it, and take positive action. This can be summarized by the initials TFA — Think, Feel, Act. Recovery demands rational thinking, recognition and management of emotions, and the ability to take constructive action and resist self-defeating impulses.

STAGE V
LATE RECOVERY

Late recovery starts after the recovering person has begun to develop effective relationships at home, work, and with friends both in and out of A.A. or other Twelve Step programs. In spite of these positive changes, many recovering people still feel unhappy. The cause of their unhappiness is often problems that began when they were children in a dysfunctional family.

Late recovery is a time to resolve family-of-origin issues in order to get free of limitations that were created in childhood. People may now say to themselves, *I have been affected by my*

18

childhood. *The quality of my recovery is not what it could be because I am blindly repeating self-defeating habits I learned as a child.*

Many recovering people resolve their family-of-origin problems very quickly and without a great deal of pain; they are able to approach adult living without being affected by irrational childhood beliefs or painful, unwanted feelings. For others, the process is more difficult. As they reconstruct their family history, they see more clearly the emotional, physical, or sexual abuse they suffered as children. Others discover that they never developed the skills necessary for positive, trusting relationships. For these people, late recovery can take as long as one to two years and can require the assistance of a trained psychotherapist.

Many recovering people indirectly resolve family issues by working the spiritual program in Steps Eleven and Twelve.

Step Eleven: Sought through prayer and meditation to improve our conscious contact with God *as we understood Him,* praying only for knowledge of His will for us and the power to carry that out.

We took time each day to focus our mind on the meaning and purpose of our lives and our sobriety. As a result, we found a new source of courage, strength, and hope within us.

Step Twelve: Having had a spiritual awakening as the result of these steps, we tried to carry this message to alcoholics, and to practice these principles in all our affairs.

We had a fundamental change in our values, thoughts, and feelings. We discovered that alcohol and other drug use was no longer important or desirable. We developed a new understanding of our addiction and the role it played in our lives. We began to feel serene and secure in ourselves and our sobriety. These new changes allowed us to help other addicted people who were still suffering. We renewed our commitment to practice a daily recovery program to assure that we wouldn't lose the gains we had made.

For most people, family-of-origin problems will linger on unless they are specifically addressed. The Twelve Step program called Adult Children Of Alcoholics (ACOA) can help. Many recovering chemically dependent people with many years of sobriety, through working an ACOA program in addition to their A.A. program, resolved their childhood issues and improved the overall quality of their recovery. The steps most recovering people take in resolving family-of-origin issues are as follows:

1. Recognizing the Effects of Childhood Problems on Sobriety

People come to realize that many problems in recovery are the result of their acting out self-defeating patterns that they learned as children. At first, they describe their problems as "one thing after another," but as their recovery progresses they begin to see that they are really having the same problems over and over. They begin to see that the only way out is to examine their childhood history to discover the attitudes they unconsciously learned. This knowledge allows them to make responsible decisions about which attitudes and habits they want to keep. They begin to see a basic rule of growth: *recover or repeat.*

- *Recover* by identifying and changing self-defeating habits learned early on, or

- *Repeat* the cycle by pretending those habits don't exist, and blaming the consequences on someone else.

2. Learning about Family-of-Origin Issues

Just as a person must learn accurate information about addiction before recovery becomes possible, people in late recovery must learn how childhood experiences affect the quality of sobriety. Most people in late recovery discover that they learned basic beliefs about themselves, other people, and the world from their

20

parents. The most powerful learning occurs before the age of five when children are not capable of evaluating what they are taught. Children unconsciously learn attitudes and habits by imitating their parents. This blind and repetitive imitation develops strong and deeply ingrained attitudes, beliefs, and habits. If parents model effective patterns of thinking, feeling, and behaving, they help their children approach life with a solid foundation for happiness and success. If, however, the parents model self-defeating patterns, children approach life with a tendency to repeat those self-defeating patterns.

3. Conscious Examination of Childhood

Knowing that self-defeating attitudes and behaviors were created during childhood is not enough to initiate change. Recovery requires the conscious examination of childhood. People do this by constructing a detailed history and talking about it with others, who then give feedback.

The process is similar to telling one's story at A.A meetings. When a person talks about painful past experiences with alcohol and drugs, a new understanding emerges. Painful memories are uncovered, talked about, and resolved. Shame and guilt subside, and a person becomes free of the past. Although the destructive events associated with active addiction are still remembered, they no longer have the power to hurt the person.

This same process is applied to problems from childhood. The recovering person writes his or her history of childhood experiences. This history is explained to others who will ask questions and give feedback. As a result, a person can develop a new understanding.

People can see how the mistaken notions they learned as children have affected their lives. Painful memories are recalled and shared with others. The pain and hurt is released and resolved. A new sense of freedom is discovered.

4. Application to Adult Living

Recovering people need to connect what they learned about childhood to adult lives. This is done by making a list of strengths and weaknesses that they brought from childhood. A plan can be made to build upon strengths and overcome weaknesses.

5. Change in Lifestyle

Finally, it is time to actually make the changes in old patterns of thinking, feeling, and acting that are identified. Deeply ingrained habits will not disappear simply because people understand how they developed. But with that understanding, recovering people become free to change. This requires setting goals, developing a plan of action, and enlisting the support of others.

STAGE VI
MAINTENANCE

The last part of the recovery process is *maintenance*. Recovering people must maintain an awareness of their chemical dependency, take a daily personal inventory, and correct problems as they develop. They need a strong commitment to continued growth. The nature of recovery is to grow, or risk relapse. Recovery is a lifelong process.

Maintenance begins when recovering people recognize they have found freedom from the past. They are no longer crippled by pain, guilt, and shame about their addiction. They have begun to be free of the self-defeating habits they learned in childhood. They are free to grow. Now the focus of recovery shifts to finding a high quality of life.

Spiritual growth and better relationships with other people become important. Most recovering people now want to pay special attention to Steps Ten, Eleven, and Twelve. The Twelve Step program of A.A. leads recovering people to search out their unique meaning and purpose. The steps they take to do this are:

1. Maintain a Recovery Program

Maintenance never ends. The disease is alcohol-ism, not alcohol-wasm. It goes into remission, but it is never "cured." Without active and continuous spiritual growth, most chemically dependent people will fall back into addictive thinking, emotional mismanagement, and self-defeating behavior. No matter how long they are sober, these problems can set the stage for relapse.

2. Effective Day-to-Day Coping

Life in recovery is not problem-free, but now recovering people have the skills to handle their problems. One A.A. member put it this way: "Recovery is nothing but a series of problems strung end to end. We are never free of problems. Recovery for me seems to be trading in one set of problems for a better set of problems. I measure my recovery not by *how many* problems I have, but by *how well* I manage them."

3. Continued Growth and Development

The human mind, when free from alcohol or other drugs, is designed to seek truth. People continue to grow and change from the time they are conceived until the time they die. They are not free to choose whether this happens; they are only free to choose the direction of growth and change. For recovering people, positive change means they need to pay constant attention to details. Change means consciously choosing thoughts, coping with feelings, and managing behavior. People accept human fallibility, and continue to do the best they can with what they have.

4. Effective Coping with Life Transitions

All people change throughout a lifetime. The first half of life is usually considered a time when people want to learn about the

23

world and things outside themselves. During the second half of life, people generally turn the focus on themselves, taking a spiritual journey of self-discovery. They reflect on the meaning of life and their place in it. In maintenance, people begin to learn about maturity. They anticipate changes they will undergo as they get older. They accept each change. They gracefully surrender the ways of youth while embracing maturity.

COPING WITH STUCK POINTS IN RECOVERY

The Big Book of Alcoholics Anonymous tells us that it is unwise to expect perfect adherence to a recovery program. The statement reads: "We claim spiritual progress rather than spiritual perfection."* It is important to recognize that every recovering person will periodically get "stuck." Getting stuck in recovery is neither good nor bad; it simply is. It is perfectly normal for recovering people to encounter problems they can't or don't know how to cope with. How they handle these situations is what makes the difference in whether they continue in recovery, or relapse.

Successfully Coping

People who continue to recover successfully cope with their stuck points through a process that can be remembered by using the acronym RADAR.

*   The first "R" stands for *recognize.* Recognize means you are aware that there is a problem and you are stuck.
*   The first "A" stands for *accept.* You accept it's normal that you have a problem and are stuck; there is no reason to be ashamed or guilty.

---

* *Alcoholics Anonymous,* Third Edition (New York: A.A. World Services, Inc., 1976), 60.

- **"D" stands for _detach._** When recovering people can't solve a problem alone, they can only make things worse by going over the same ground again and again. People who succeed in recovery back off to gain perspective, and they turn their problem over to a Power greater than themselves.

- The second **"A" stands for _accept help_** — being able to reach out to others for help. Recovering people turn to a Higher Power for courage, strength, and hope, and to other people for help and support.

- The final **"R" stands for _respond with action._** Problems don't just go away; they need our attention. People who succeed in recovery take positive action toward getting unstuck.

Unsuccessfully Coping

People with low quality sobriety, some of whom eventually relapse, cope with their stuck points by evading or denying problems. This creates stress which they deny or blame on someone or something else. Stress often fuels other compulsive behaviors such as overeating, overworking, overexercising, compulsive sexuality, or codependent relationships. These compulsive behaviors might relieve stress in the short run, but overall they weaken people. They might feel good now, but they will hurt later. As a result of substituting addictions, stress symptoms develop and grow more severe.

Instead of detaching from the problem and seeking outside help, some people lock onto and hide the problem. This encourages isolation from other people. Problems are denied and evaded. This can be described by using an acronym ESCAPE.

- The first **"E" is for _evasion_ and denial** of the stuck point or problem.

- **"S" is the _stress_ that follows.** The human mind tends to seek truth or reality. Any time we deny reality, we must turn off our minds. It is very stressful to do this.

25

- "C" is *compulsive behavior*. Stress can lead to compulsive behavior that distracts from uncomfortable feelings.
- "A" is *avoidance of others*. The conflicts from stress and compulsive behaviors alienate other people. A person coping (or not coping) in this way remains isolated and alone.
- "P" is for *problems*. New problems are the natural result of stress, compulsive behavior, and isolation.
- The final "E" is for *evasion and denial of new problems*. This starts the self-defeating cycle, and each time it is repeated, it drains a person's energy. The ability to cope with life is impaired.

THE RELAPSE PROCESS

The bottom half of *The Relapse/Recovery Grid* summarizes the common progression of warning signs that lead to relapse. Not all people who relapse experience all of the signs, but most can recognize this general pattern of progressive dysfunction.

The general direction toward relapse is from *denial and evasion* to *high-risk lifestyle factors*. These high-risk factors don't cause relapse; they simply increase the likelihood that it will occur. (Being overweight doesn't cause a heart attack, but it does increase the risk.) These high-risk factors were identified from research into lifestyles of people who relapse.

High-risk factors make people vulnerable to *trigger events*. A trigger event is anything that causes sudden stress, pain, or discomfort. Trigger events can be internal or external. Common internal trigger events include

- self-defeating or irrational thoughts,
- painful emotions, or
- painful unresolved memories.

Common external trigger events are

- high-stress situations, and
- stressful interactions with other people.

26

The relationship between the number of high-risk factors and the intensity of the trigger event determines whether or not a person begins to malfunction. With few high-risk factors in people's lives, it will take a greater stressor to trigger internal dysfunction. The opposite is also true. With more high-risk factors, it may take a minor event to trigger internal dysfunction. Sometimes, internal relapse warning signs result from a buildup of stressors interacting with a nervous system that has been damaged by long-term addictive use. As internal dysfunction increases, the ability to manage reality gets worse, and more problems develop. A vicious cycle begins. Symptoms of internal dysfunction are difficulty in

- thinking clearly,

- managing emotions,

- remembering things,

- sleeping restfully,

- managing stress, and

- being accident prone (shown on the grid as difficulty with physical coordination).

This internal dysfunction has been described as *post-acute* or *protracted withdrawal.*

The presence of internal warning signs does not mean people will relapse. Internal warning signs set the stage for relapse only when they are denied, ignored, or poorly managed.

As these internal problems worsen, external problems develop too. People who don't function well internally have difficulty functioning externally. An example of external dysfunction is people whose daily schedules are so chaotic that they miss appointments. People may stop making plans entirely, because they can't be sure they will follow through. Eventually, problems erupt with their families, friends, jobs, and in their recovery programs. This creates more stress, and eventually they may lose control of a responsible daily routine entirely.

27

Finally, there comes *loss of control* over judgment and behavior. Consistent self-defeating behaviors increase pain and further interfere with people's ability to function. Options are reduced so people believe they have only three choices: self-medication through alcohol and other drug use, physical and/or emotional collapse, or suicide. With only these apparent choices, many chemically dependent people feel that self-medication is the sane and reasonable option, and they return to drinking or using other drugs.

The constant use of denial and evasion, the ESCAPE strategy, weakens people in the long run. As they begin to burn out, their personality changes create conflicts and instability in relationships. Health problems, from chronic fatigue to a major illness, can develop. People may begin to neglect their recovery program because they feel too sick and tired to keep working at it.

We will now review this relapse progression in more detail.

HIGH-RISK FACTORS

1. High-Stress Personality*

Often, people with high-stress personalities are at war with themselves and others. They tend to be critical of both themselves and others, and generally dissatisfied with sobriety. They often punish themselves and push themselves to be perfect. This personality style is often described as *Type A*. Type A behavior not only sets the stage for relapse, but it increases the risk of heart disease, cancer, and other stress-related illnesses. The high-stress personality type usually creates a high-stress lifestyle.

---

* Editor's note: The concepts discussed for each area in the relapse progression are numbered to correspond with *The Relapse/Recovery Grid.*

28

2. High-Risk Lifestyle

A high-risk lifestyle is marked by too much, too little, or the wrong kind. People who fill their lives with too many activities and responsibilities feel stress and frustration. They simply cannot get everything done. People who fill their lives with too few activities suffer from the stress of boredom. People who fill their lives with the wrong things can feel stress from disillusionment and frustration. The "wrong things" could be occupations, activities, and people that don't fit with natural preferences and talents. When recovering people live with continuous, unrelieved stress, they create conflict and instability in relationships with other people.

3. Social Conflict or Change

People get along with others by acting appropriately within their roles as spouses, employees, parents, and friends, and many others as well. But high stress may cause people to act in inappropriate ways that create conflict in relationships. As the conflicts grow worse, relationships are strained.

4. Poor Health Maintenance

Proper nutrition, exercise, relaxation, and socializing are all necessary to a healthy lifestyle. As stress and high-risk factors accumulate, many recovering people revert to bad eating habits (such as skipping meals and eating junk food), lack of exercise, and constant work with little or no time devoted to recreation and relaxation. Many people ignore their health and refuse to seek medical care when necessary. They ignore headaches and back-aches. They ignore weight gain and symptoms of stress. They continue to work right through colds and flu. This lack of proper health maintenance further weakens them.

5   Other Illness

While heading toward relapse, it's common for recovering people to get sick. Chronic fatigue periodically gives way to colds, flu, and headaches. This happens because their chronic stress is weakening the immune systems. Their bodies are losing the ability to fight germs and viruses. As people get more fatigued, weaker, and sicker, it is difficult to maintain a recovery program.

6.   Inadequate Recovery Program

An early sign of an inadequate recovery program is boredom or complacency. Other warning signs are problems that cannot be handled. At this stage, people begin to feel that their recovery program is either unnecessary or isn't working very well. They begin to practice what is described in the Big Book of Alcoholics Anonymous as "half measures" — the tendency to do the minimum necessary to get by.

The accumulation of more and more of these risk factors lowers resistance to stressors. The more risk factors present, the less stress it takes to trigger internal dysfunction.

TRIGGER EVENTS

Some recovering people put themselves under increasing amounts of stress, and they keep adapting to it as they go along. As their tolerance goes up, they block their awareness of stress. Suddenly, they hit their limit. They experience one stressor too many, and they become dysfunctional.

Just about anything can be a trigger event, but five things tend to trigger internal dysfunction more than others.

1. High-Stress Thoughts

The most common trigger is irrational thinking. Something goes wrong, and the person thinks, *Nothing ever goes right!* This thought is irrational. Some things do go right. But thinking that nothing ever goes right leads people to believe they are failures.

2. Painful Emotions

Emotions are neither good nor bad; they simply are. All emotions, pleasant and painful, serve a function. Physical pain tells people there is something wrong with their bodies. Emotional pain can point to something wrong with how people are thinking and acting. Emotional pain signals a need to examine what is wrong. When people dismiss painful emotions for long, the feelings often come back with a vengeance. Many recovering people suppress painful feelings and suddenly, during a period of fatigue, they are overwhelmed with fear, anxiety, depression, or sadness.

3. Painful Memories

People often experience events in their life that cause extreme emotional or physical pain. Perhaps they were physically assaulted, raped, injured in a serious accident, fought in a war, et cetera. When severe physical or emotional trauma occurs, the conscious mind, often unable to deal with it, may temporarily "shut down." Often, the memory of such traumas is expressed as muscle tension within the body. This is called an *unresolved memory.*
Whenever a person is reminded of the unresolved experience, symptoms develop. The reminder may be a sight, sound, touch, or smell that is similar to the experience. Common symptoms are feeling spacy, confused, and disoriented, or feeling anxious for no apparent reason. These symptoms increase stress, and internal dysfunction is triggered. People need to relieve this stress by

discussing the experience in detail with another person who will listen, understand, take seriously, and acknowledge the experience. When this happens, the pain is discharged, and the stress is then reduced.

4. Stressful Situations

Any situation that a person is not prepared to cope with may be stressful. For example, a recovering woman went to a staff meeting at work. Her boss suddenly asked her to give a public presentation on a project she had been working on. She had no idea she was going to be asked to make the presentation, and experienced such severe stress she was unable to give the report. She was then asked to prepare the report for a later meeting. Because she had adequate time to prepare, she was calm enough to effectively deliver her report. The level of stress in this situation goes down as the level of preparation goes up. To lower stress, we need to increase our level of preparation.

5. Stressful Interactions With Other People

A supervisor once told me, "I don't get ulcers, I give them." He was a very high stress person. Those around him felt stress just being in his presence. Many recovering people report having high-stress people in their lives. The stress of interacting with these people is often enough to trigger internal dysfunction, especially when a person is tired.

INTERNAL DYSFUNCTION

When under high stress, many recovering people begin to have difficulty thinking clearly, managing feelings and emotions, and remembering things. One of the main culprits leading to these problems appears to be a tendency to overreact to stressors. Scientists call this neurological augmentation. Many recovering people refer to this as stress sensitivity. People perceive light to be brighter, sound to be louder, and touch to be intrusive. They startle easily and quickly, and become distracted by things that happen around them. Eventually, the ability to sleep restfully is disrupted. This heightens stress and fatigue to the point where people become accident-prone.

1. Difficulty in Thinking Clearly

Recovering people often have trouble thinking clearly or solving usually simple problems. At times, their minds race with rigid and repetitive thoughts; at other times, their minds seem to shut down or go blank. They have difficulty concentrating or thinking logically for more than a few minutes. As a result, they are not always sure about how one thing relates to or affects other things. They have difficulty deciding what to do next to manage their lives and recovery.

2. Difficulty in Managing Feelings and Emotions

During periods of recovery, many recovering people may over-react emotionally (feel too much). At other times, they may become emotionally numb (feel too little), or unable to know what they are feeling. At still other times, they may feel strange or "crazy feelings" for no apparent reason, and think they are going crazy. These problems in managing feelings can cause recovering people to experience mood swings, depression, anxiety, and fear. As a result, they don't trust their emotions and often try to ignore them, stuff them, or forget about them.

3. Difficulty in Remembering Things

Many recovering people have memory problems that prevent them from learning new information and skills. The new things they learn dissolve or evaporate from their mind within minutes. They also have problems remembering key events from their childhood, adolescence, or adulthood. At times, they remember things clearly; at other times, these same memories will not come to mind. They feel blocked, or cut off from these memories.

4. Difficulty in Sleeping Restfully

During certain periods of recovery, many people have difficulty sleeping restfully. Either they cannot fall asleep, or, when they do sleep, they have unusual or disturbing dreams. They may awaken many times and have difficulty falling asleep again. They rarely experience a deep, relaxing sleep. They may awaken feeling tired. At times, they stay up late because they can't fall asleep, and oversleep because they are too tired to get up. At times, they become so exhausted they sleep for extremely long periods, sometimes sleeping around the clock for one or more days.

5. Difficulty in Managing Stress

Difficulty in managing stress is caused by a combination of two factors.

The first factor is the brain dysfunction caused by long-term alcohol or other drug poisoning. Although much of this dysfunction will eventually be reversed, recovery takes time. It is estimated that recovering people will experience one month of stress sensitivity for each year of active addiction.

When the brain becomes overloaded, it shuts down temporarily. Most electrical devices such as toasters and stereos have fuses. The job of the fuse is to shut off the device if the current is too high. The brain appears to have its own fuse. When the stress level becomes too high, the brain shuts down temporarily. The first symptom of this is a shutdown of the ability to experience feelings: emotional numbness.

34

When emotionally numb, recovering people cannot recognize the minor signs of daily stress. When the stress does manage to break into their consciousness, they tend to overreact. The stress sensitivity causes them to amplify, magnify, and intensify whatever feeling they are experiencing. Even when they do recognize stress, they are unable to relax. The things people normally do to relax either don't work for them or actually make the stress worse. They get so tense that they are not in control of themselves. At times, the strain is so severe that they can't function normally.

6. Difficulty with Physical Coordination

Sometimes recovering people have difficulty with coordination that results in dizziness, balance problems, or slow reflexes. These problems create clumsiness or make them prone to accidents.

7. Shame, Guilt, and Hopelessness

At times, some recovering people feel a deep sense of shame because they believe they are crazy, emotionally disturbed, defective, or incapable of being normal. At other times, they feel guilty because they believe they are doing something wrong or not working a good program. The shame and guilt often cause them to hide warning signs of relapse and stop talking honestly with others about what they are experiencing. The longer they keep their problems hidden, the stronger the warning signs become. They try to manage these internal warning signs alone, but fail. They begin to feel hopeless.

8. Return of Denial

During this phase of internal dysfunction, recovering people become unable to recognize and honestly tell others what they are thinking or feeling. They block the concern about their well-being from their mind and forget about it. They make themselves believe everything is fine. Many people deny sobriety-based problems the same way they denied their addiction. Even when they are aware of their feelings, they often forget them. Only when they reflect on the situation can they recognize their feelings of anxiety.

EXTERNAL DYSFUNCTION

When this warning sign appears, recovering people begin to have serious life problems. Before this, problems were internal and easily ignored and hidden. Now problems arise at work, at home, with friends, and with fellow members of the program. These problems begin with avoidance and defensive behavior; they lead to crisis building, and culminate in confusion, overreaction, and depression.

1. Avoidance and Defensive Behavior

Here, recovering people don't want to think about anything that will interrupt their denial and cause painful feelings to come back. As a result, they begin to avoid anything or anybody that will force them to take an honest look at themselves. When asked questions about their well-being, they may become defensive.

During this period, it is not unusual for people to convince themselves they will never drink or use other drugs again. They may begin to worry more about others than they do about themselves. In A.A., this is called "working someone else's program." When people are asked to think or talk about themselves, they may become defensive. They distract themselves from doing this with compulsive behavior. They often act impulsively, doing things without thought or self-control. These impulsive actions cause them to make decisions that seriously damage their life and recovery. They begin to spend a lot of time alone and feel isolated. Instead of confronting the loneliness by being around others, they become more compulsive and impulsive.

36

2. Crisis Building

Here, people may begin to have problems caused by denying their feelings, isolating themselves, and neglecting their recovery. Even though they might want to solve their problems and work hard at it, two new problems pop up to replace every one they do solve. Each crisis is a symptom of progression toward relapse, not the real problem. When recovering people become preoccupied with solving individual problems without seeing how they fit into the context of their addiction, they seldom make progress. They solve problem "A" only to face problem "B." As they solve problem "B," problem "C" rears its ugly head. The process is called *symptom substitution*. The real problem is that they are setting themselves up for addictive use.

3. Immobilization

Symptoms of depression appear and persist. People may feel down, blue, listless, empty of feelings. Oversleeping becomes common. They are able to distract themselves by getting busy with other things. Depression interferes with their ability to make plans. They may misinterpret the A.A. slogan, One Day at a Time, to mean that they shouldn't plan or think about what they are going to do. Less and less attention is paid to detail. Plans are based on wishful thinking more than on reality, and each failure triggers a new crisis.

4. Confusion and Overreaction

Here, recovering people are confused. They may become upset with themselves and others. They are irritable and overreact to small things. The periods of confusion are more frequent, last longer, and cause more problems. The recovering people experiencing this often feel angry with themselves because of their inability to understand things. Relationships become strained with friends, family, counselors, and Twelve Step group members. They may feel threatened when others talk about changes. Conflicts increase. They feel guilty and remorseful. They experience anger, frustration, and resentment. Stress and anxiety increase because they fear their overreacting to things might result in violence.

5. Depression

Here, recovering people become so depressed they have difficulty following normal routines. At times, they may contemplate suicide, drinking, or drug use as a way to end the depression. The depression is severe and persistent; it cannot be easily ignored or hidden from others. They may begin overeating and gain weight; or they may undereat and lose weight. They lose consistency in their daily structure. Appointments are missed. Responsibilities are neglected. They stop eating regular meals, and replace a well-balanced, nourishing diet with "junk food."

There are periods when they are unable to get started or to get anything done. They cannot concentrate; they feel anxious, fearful, and trapped with no way out. They have serious difficulty sleeping and are restless and fitful when they do sleep. They begin to have strange and frightening dreams. It's not unusual for them to collapse from exhaustion and sleep for twelve to twenty-four hours at a time.

LOSS OF CONTROL

When this warning sign appears, recovering people lose their ability to control their thinking and behavior. Judgment is impaired. They often know what they need to do but can't do it. They begin having cravings and self-destructive impulses and find them more and more difficult to resist. They consciously recognize the loss of control, but believe they can't do anything about it.

1. Poor Judgment

Judgment is the capacity to recognize the logical consequences of behavior and act accordingly. Recovering people who are out of control show terrible judgment. This poor judgment may prompt them to stop attending A.A., or miss counseling appointments. They find reasons that justify this. They think, *A.A. and counseling don't make me feel better, so why should I make them a priority? Other things are more important.* They act as if they don't care about their problems. They hide their feelings of helplessness and their growing lack of self-respect and confidence. Things seem so bad that they think that they might as well use mood-altering chemicals again, because things couldn't get worse. Life has become unmanageable since drinking or using other drugs has stopped.

2. Inability to Take Action

Recovering people may go through the motions of living, but are controlled by life rather than controlling it. The "if only" syndrome becomes more common in conversation. They have fantasies of escaping, or of being rescued by an event unlikely to happen. Daydreaming and wishful thinking replace realistic planning.

They believe there is no hope. They think, *I've tried my best and recovery isn't working out.* They may feel a vague desire to be happy or to have things work out without doing the necessary legwork.

3. Inability to Resist Destructive Impulses

Cravings come back and, with them, the urges to act out in self-destructive or self-defeating ways. People know they shouldn't give in to these urges, but they feel weak and tired. They remember how good it felt to use alcohol and other drugs and act irresponsibly. They block out or ignore the memory of the pain they felt. They irrationally think that addictive use is better than sobriety.

4. Conscious Recognition of the Severity of Loss of Control

Their denial breaks, and they suddenly recognize how severe their problems are, how unmanageable life has become, and how little power and control they have to solve the problems. This awareness is very painful and frightening. By this time, they have become so isolated that it seems there is no one to turn to for help. They begin to feel sorry for themselves and may use self-pity to get attention.

They realize that drinking or using drugs would help them to feel better. They begin to hope that they can drink or use normally again and be able to control it. Sometimes, they can put these thoughts out of their mind, but often the thoughts are so strong that they can't be stopped. People may begin to believe that drinking is the only alternative to going crazy or committing suicide. Drinking or other drug use actually looks like a sane and rational alternative.

They recognize the lying, denial, and excuses, but are unable to stop. They feel trapped and overwhelmed by the inability to think clearly or take action. This feeling of powerlessness causes them to believe they are useless and incompetent. As a result, they believe they can't manage life. They completely lose self-confidence and self-worth.

5. Option Reduction

Here, recovering people feel trapped by the pain and inability to manage life. The only ways out appear to be insanity, suicide, or addictive use. They no longer believe anyone or anything can help them. They feel angry because they can't control their behavior. Sometimes, their anger is with the world, sometimes it's with someone or something in particular, and sometimes it's with themselves. They stop attending Twelve Step meetings entirely. Tension may become so severe that the relationship with a sponsor or helper ends. They may drop out of professional counseling. Feeling completely overwhelmed, they may have an intense fear of insanity. This progressive and disabling loss of control causes serious problems in every area of life and begins to affect one's health.

6. Emotional or Physical Collapse

Sometimes, recovering people have such a strong commitment to sobriety, they would rather die than begin addictive use again. Some may hang on, taking it One Day at a Time, and get back into an effective recovery program. Others do not.

People can only live with debilitating stress for so long before they collapse. Some people collapse physically and develop stress-related illnesses such as ulcers, gastritis, back pain, heart disease, or cancer. Others collapse emotionally. They find that they cannot cope. Still others become suicidal, believing that life is not worth living. Many attempt suicide.

LAPSE/RELAPSE

1. Initial Use of Alcohol or Other Drugs

Some recovering people realize that these symptoms of internal and external dysfunction and loss of control can be temporarily medicated by alcohol or drug use. When faced with the limited alternatives of physical or emotional collapse, suicide, or chemical use, using can seem like the sanest choice. At this point, many recovering people are so desperate that they make themselves believe that controlled use is possible. They plan to use for a short time in a controlled way.

2. Severe Shame, Guilt, and Remorse

Initial use produces feelings of intense guilt and shame. Guilt is the feeling caused by the self-judgment, *I have done something wrong*. The recently relapsed person feels morally responsible for the return to use and believes it wouldn't have happened if he or she had done the right things. Shame is the feeling caused by the self-judgment, *I am a defective person*. Many recovering people feel their relapse proves they are worthless and that they might as well die using.

3. Loss of Control over Use

The addictive use spirals out of control. Sometimes that loss of control occurs slowly. At other times the loss of control is rapid, with the person using as often and as much as before.

4. Development of Health and Life Problems

People who relapse may have severe problems with their life and health. Marriage, jobs, and friendships are seriously damaged. Physical health suffers and they become so ill that they need professional treatment. In the end, chemically dependent people who relapse will face a single choice — to stop using and get back into recovery, or to die. This is the nature of chemical addiction. We must either live sober or die.

CONCLUSION

So what is this journey of recovery? What is the pathway to success? What is the road to failure? Hopefully, this pamphlet has helped you to answer those questions.

Recovery is a process that unfolds in six major stages. It begins with *Transition* — we become aware of the problems caused by our alcohol and other drug use, make repeated efforts to control our use, and fail. Eventually, we admit defeat and become ready to totally abstain from alcohol and other mood-altering drugs.

We then move into *Stabilization.* We discover that abstinence isn't easy. We can't do it alone. We seek help in overcoming both short-term and long-term withdrawal, managing the crises that follow us into sobriety, and developing effective problem-solving strategies.

As we stabilize, we enter *Early Recovery,* where we begin to consciously sort out our alcohol and drug use history, understand our addiction, and make sense out of what has happened to us and to those we love. We learn to accept our addiction and resolve the feelings of guilt, shame, and nagging pain associated with our addiction.

Then we move on into *Middle Recovery,* where we repair past damage caused by our addiction and move ahead to establish a balanced lifestyle. This prepares us for *Late Recovery,* where we identify problems originating in childhood that are lowering the quality of our recovery. We work at resolving those problems. This takes us into the final stage — *Maintenance.* Here, we move ahead to live a meaningful and comfortable life without the need for alcohol or other drugs. We remain aware of our disease and the possibility of relapse.

Recovery is a lifelong journey through a passage that is often dark and strewn with obstacles. Many people get stuck at various stages. Those who successfully continue in recovery recognize that they are stuck, accept that it's okay, and detach from the immediate problem long enough to get help. They then respond with action and move ahead in their recovery.

Those who relapse get trapped in denial and evasion. When they get stuck, they refuse to admit it. They attempt to hide their problems, experience stress, and generally try to cope by using some other compulsive behavior to distract themselves. They become isolated and their problems spiral out of control. Eventually, they become so desperate that they believe they have only three choices — suicide, physical or emotional collapse, or chemical use.

It's Our Choice

Recovering people have a choice. We can determine which of these passages we take. Do we move ahead in our recovery, or do we lapse back to chemical use, or worse?

Having a road map doesn't guarantee that we'll get to our final destination, but it does improve our chances. It's my sincere hope the road map to recovery that I have described in this pamphlet will be helpful in your personal journey, or in your ability to help others along the way.

Remember, recovery is nothing but a series of problems strung end to end. We are never free of problems. Recovery is a process of trading in one set of problems for a better set of problems. Successful recovery isn't measured by how many problems we have, but by how well we manage them. May you manage your problems successfully.

APPENDIX ONE

THE TWELVE STEPS
OF ALCOHOLICS ANONYMOUS*

1. We admitted we were powerless over alcohol — that our lives had become unmanageable.
2. Came to believe that a Power greater than ourselves could restore us to sanity.
3. Made a decision to turn our will and our lives over to the care of God *as we understood Him.*
4. Made a searching and fearless moral inventory of ourselves.
5. Admitted to God, to ourselves, and to another human being the exact nature of our wrongs.
6. Were entirely ready to have God remove all these defects of character.
7. Humbly asked Him to remove our shortcomings.
8. Made a list of all persons we had harmed, and became willing to make amends to them all.
9. Made direct amends to such people wherever possible, except when to do so would injure them or others.
10. Continued to take personal inventory and when we were wrong promply admitted it.
11. Sought through prayer and meditation to improve our conscious contact with God *as we understood Him,* praying only for knowledge of His will for us and the power to carry that out.
12. Having had a spiritual awakening as the result of these steps, we tried to carry this message to alcoholics, and to practice these principles in all our affairs.

---

* The Twelve Steps are taken from *Alcoholics Anonymous* (Third Edition), published by A.A. World Services, Inc., New York, N.Y., 59-60. Reprinted with permission.

Expand Your Knowledge with These Materials . . .

Passages through Recovery
An Action Plan for Preventing Relapse
by Terence T. Gorski
   This pioneering work from Terence T. Gorski describes six stages of recovery from chemical dependency and offers sound advice for working through the challenges of each stage. 125 pp.
Order No. 5052

Dual Disorders
Counseling Clients with
Chemical Dependency and Mental Illness
by Dennis C. Daley, M.S.W., Howard Moss, M.D., and Frances Campbell, M.S.N.
   Increase your awareness of the most common psychiatric disorders found in alcoholics with this comprehensive guide. One of the first books to address the needs which exist in this area of treatment.
Order No. 1963

Sponsor p 8
radar p24
escape p25

HazELDEN®

hazelden.org
800-328-9000

ISBN 978-0-89486-544-2
90000

Order No. 5198